Colored Raindrops

Echoes of the Soul

by
Jess L. Martinez

Colored Raindrops
Echoes of the Soul

Copyright © 2002 by Jess L. Martinez

All rights reserved under International and Pan-American copyright conventions. No part of this book may be reproduced, stored in a retrieval system or transmitted in any form, electronic, mechanical or by other means, without written permission of the author.

Library of Congress
Cataloging in Publication Data

ISBN 0-7951-0332-8

Manufactured in The United States of America by
Watermark Press
6 Gwynns Mill Court
Owings Mills, MD 21117
410-654-0400

Table of Contents

Moments Of The Heart
I Love You Too
Love Once Broken
Poetic Proclamation
Bird
That Moment
The Walk
A Warm, Warm Hug
"Right-On-Charm"
I Shed No Tears
Bread
Green-Eyed Lady
Two Thousand Miles
A Blanket To The Poor

Awakenings Of The Soul
Uneasy Rhythm
Rich In Tradition
Laid Out
A Crescent Moon
Birth
180 Degrees
Crystal Flakes
"That"
That Light
Enamored
Cognition
The Garden
The Knock

Plight
Ha!
Reaching
Enjoy
As I Write
Dust

Gray Notes
I Closed My Eyes
Grow Old And Die
I Too Have Been Forgotten
The End
Wild Grass
My Wash
Scheme Of Things
The Cloud

A Sigh Of Love
A Special Graduation
My Momma
Tempered Patience
Ponytailed Lass
She Touched The Sky
Three Joys
Beauty
That Feline
She Traveled Far

Moments Of The Heart

Funtasia
Remember
All In One Act
"I'll Tell You What!"
Colored Rocks
Marbles
Monopoly
Space
Long Ago
Steel Glass Murals
Volcano Warm
Nurtured In An Earth Tradition

Mixed Strokes
Baby
Kurillo's Juniper
Unforeseen
The Spirit
Rags Of Silk
Ever-present
Freedom
Nay To All!
My Love
Two Larks

Freedoms Grace
America United
Shadows In Our Land
Irish Noble Blood
Offerings

"I Love You Too!"

I flew the untamed currents
in a dream world in my mind
I was floating like a feather
and was reaching for the sky.

No one there to say, "You cannot do that!"
No one there to stop my thriving
And I went up past our heaven
to where God's hand touches mine.

We talked and prayed for good things
High aesthetics rich in love
Then I woke up in the morning
Feeling light like a balloon

My sweet mother said, "Good Morning!"
And I said "I LOVE YOU TOO!"

Love Once Broken

The eyes that I adore avoid me
when I connect they speak and say
"Where did you go?" "Why didn't you stay?"
profound and longing
...whisper of love once broken

How deep's a well? How high's the sky?
How can you keep those eyes from
gazing into mine? And when I feel
your eyes in mine
...a tinge of love once broken

Your fragrance penetrates my being
the essence of your very soul mingles
with my own; no need to touch as I cognite
the beauty in your heart
...the depth of love once broken

This love we'll always have, though
you belong to someone else, our bonding
holds eternal. Don't sin by seeking out
my flesh; be firm, survive!
...the cycle of love once broken

February 20, 2000

Poetic Proclamation

Like a town crier
she gave her words
to all who would listen
Like a great artist
whose words stand out
bold, profound,
aching to be discovered
and like a good food
devoured...
Her pay, a morsel dish
of water soup.
Yet, in her heart a glint
of Godly Inspiration devoted
to Creation of Poetic Proclamation
just like a Spiritual Incantation
of words...
that sing and move with rhythm
to your heart's enjoyment
and her soul's courting
with God.

Bird

Upon a Wave
I soared
as the wind
caressed my cheeks
I felt loved
spiritually creative
and a conqueror
I sailed
not breathing
nor looking
yet seeing
I climbed to God
and said
Thanks!

June 27, 2000

That Moment

Often I can see better at night
And as the light cool breeze
Caresses my cheeks I remember,
Like one would a loved memory,
A treasured and well-kept moment.
That time when you asked if I cared
About you in the dark
And I did not answer,
For it was not a moment for words
But expression in the purest form.
I touched your forehead,
Gently moving your hair back
And I gave you a tender kiss,
Not a dominant kiss
Nor one asking anything in return,
But a gentle, tender, unselfish kiss
That sealed your assurance
And your trust in me,
For love is a clean impeccable action;
It does not hurt, nor intend hurt.
It is plain and pure
Love!

May 10, 2000

The Walk

In the moonless night
As the crisp cool wind
Caressed my cheeks
I walked.
I could literally touch the night
And like a leaf it would crumble
In my palms,
Such was its delicate attribute
In balance with my capricious explorations.
The lack of light from above
Contrasted to the ever-glowing
Candle within my nature.
Winding dirt roads,
Unforgettable picturesque
Adobe brick homes
Full of enchantment,
Mysterious people,
Strong willed,
Hard working,
Eyes reflecting fear of unknowns.
The darkness
Was enchantingly beautiful,
It caressed my soul
And inspired my will.

I walked
Savoring the settled dust
Under my feet
While the crickets
Sang to me.
As I crossed a brook
The water spoke with flowing whispers,
An illusion
Of pure crystal clear
Underground flowing water
Filled my every sense.
As I distanced myself
From the brook
I felt my body renewed
And fresh.
In the distance
I could make the well
Where water would be drawn
Three in the morning
When witches fly,
Corn devils barter for souls,
I walked for water.
Inspiration
Filled my cup
To write that which I saw
And felt.
That was my integrity!

A crow so black
I could not see
But felt its heart and flutter of wings in the air
While a venomous snake
Slithered by
As I smiled
Wishing it good night.
On this two-mile walk
To get water
I grew strong
In my gait and my will
For I savored the crispness of night,
All its elements,
Creatures,
And most of all water,
I of seven years old
Was a man of one hundred
And a thousand past lives
As I walked,
So I knew who I was,
In this Portuguese town
Of my homeland.

April 10, 2001

A Warm, Warm Hug

Color: Beauty Waves that dress a gallant world.
Those eyes of blue,
The red in hair
And all your love
Brings color to the air.
Your candid smile
A warm, warm hug
The beauty in a newborn
Color that shines and shines!
A Poet's thought,
A Writer's pen,
One's first-found love,
The honest handshake of a friend,
Color that sparkles through and through
Color that's there,
It's meant for you!

"Right-On-Charm"

Almond eyes like charcoal beams
Enticing my participation
Seducing, well dressed, beams
Like crystal clear angelic breath
So cool, so calm
So "right-on-charm!"
A tiny body of a soul,
Weighs not much more
Than a cantaloupe;
A honeydew for sweetness,
A heart of gold for love,
And in the center of this baby
An immortal soul.

I Shed No Tears

A heartfelt song I send you dear,
upon your gray-tint bed
bouquet of roses for my love
whose mistress is at hand.
For thee I pray…and shed no tears
when in my heart I bear
such lovely memories.

August 3, 2001

Bread

A three-foot basket
Full of bread
To waiting customers
On a rainy day.
Five blocks North
Then two more South
To Chano's Market
A well-known site.
Rubber Boots sloshing
Through sticky mud
The Bread-Man's work
Is not quite done
At three in the morning
With dogs on his tracks
a basket on his head.

September 12, 2001

Green-Eyed Lady

Inventive red-haired girl,
Green-eyed Hawaiian,
Lucy would be jealous.
Knit a little
and see the Islands
in your heart,
they should be abundantly green.
Are not your fingers paths
to enchanting wells
of fountain of youth waters?
Your eyes don't lie!
they are portals
to grand adventure
and beauty!

September 14, 2001

Two Thousand Miles

Dusty, burly tired men
Calloused hands
Reaching for water
Pumping it out
From a well
In a farm.
Dead tired
They find a spot,
Sit their bodies.
They eat some,
Laugh some.
Some sing,
Others sleep.
A hard job,
A manly job!
Cattle to watch.
Two thousand miles
Pushing cows
Through chaparral
And desert
To a promised land
And pay.

A Blanket To The Poor

To shine upon this world
And cast a "Just Right" warmth
Has always been my duty
My Godly given chore.
I've often been portrayed
As a "blanket to the poor,"
A God to some, a friend to many,
I'm just a star –
No warmer than your own,
The one that's in your heart.

Awakenings Of The Soul

July 17, 2001

Uneasy Rhythm

Salty teardrops caressed my cheeks
While notes of every-growing distant thunder
Pounded my mind
As my heart, my poor breaking heart
Beat in uneasy rhythm
And, like a dramatic movie,
Scenes of careless love and joy
Flooding my senses
As distance, ever-growing distance
Severed a bond of love.
And like a day that fades into the night
Hauntingly disappearing, vanishing
I wiped my cheeks and sighed
"No More!" as the gates opened.
I drove out…out of the cemetery
And into life.

Rich In Tradition

In form and thought my body swayed
To rhythmic incantations
Coming from bamboo musical creations
In that village of Gumaro
Municipio de Quentacuaro
Played by Indian Village Natives
Dressed in white

Shetca, Metzqui, and Murita
Played to quench their inner spirits
As I danced to their sonidos
And their lyrical concatenation
Of Peruvian origination
From a time rich in tradition
Full of sound.

High on top of the Montanas
Where the air starts to thin out,
Heaven must have left her beauty
And her spirit in their hearts,
For in every tone and lyric
You'll hear messages from God
As you dance.

Laid Out

I stood there gazing at the crowd
In tones of dark and gray they prayed
Some cried, some stared,
and in the middle of this bunch
a coffin! Wonder who it was?
As I came up right through the crowd
no one objected, no one cared!
That's when I saw my body laid out…dead!

A Crescent Moon

A crescent moon I see tonight
And stars that call my name,
As I with pen write poetry
That bleeds with "love"
And thrives for "life"
Of times rich in "emotion."
White doves,
Blue Waves,
Large almond eyes
That tell no lies,
And crisp cool nights
That whisper.
Large elephants so shy
They knock on doors
And then they run.
Ha, Ha, for the Giraffe
That cooked a dinner
On the tree top!
And on a serious note,
A rose that thrives
Inside my heart
Refusing to wilt away.
And ocean's depth,
An ant-long trek,
A lost flower
Left its shade.
The rhythm in your heart
A narrative will tell,
Of light and dark,
Such chiaroscuro shade
That talks,
Making poetic sense.

Birth

In the twinkle of a moment
By the sigh of new found love
Through the mist of Ocean Magic
As Angel Wings flap in delight
Comes the first gasp of a newborn
That has brought out a few tears.
Tears of joy! Tears of love!
Salty, Caressing water drops
Drowning out the pains of birth,
With a twinkle…with a sigh
With a Mist of Ocean Magic
As the Angels frolic by.

180 Degrees

Beauty, Hah! To look in awe at some miniscule crumb of bread
Savor its dying flavor and perceive it going down
Into thirsting empty void of a stomach
That growls for lack of speech
As the world spins pleasantly
On its axis
Caring
Not
And
Waking up to
A sumptuous seven-entrée meal
In a wonderful home full of light and love
Thinking how fortunate of me, not knowing of hardship;
A full stomach that learns and grows lazy for lack of work.
Ugliness, Hah! Impossible in a godly perfect world full of love!

Crystal Flakes

I touched upon a daisy
On a starry full moon night
The dewdrops wet my hands
And woke my sensitivity,
Alas! The night was alive
And I was free to care
And I was free to love,
For within reach a rose
A cactus flower, a dandelion,
And then I saw a rainbow
In the middle of the night,
I closed my eyes
To see if it would disappear
But no, it was still there.
Its aura full of color
With crystal flakes of water
Gliding, sliding to and fro
All along the rainbow arch
When I touched upon a daisy.

"That"

Enough! Of lies that hurt,
Is not one's soul a penny worth?
Truth does not lie
Nor does it sit in wait
For you to cry,
And "that" you do
Without a tear,
And in your heart
That's full of doubt
Of doubt!
So much of "that,"
That you look out
For truth in others
Knowing full well
Stability of thought
Is that you're best at
"A game"
I say you've made of that
And in your heart
A vein, a ventricle,
A muscle pumping blood
With feelings
From the heart?
Step back!
Away for "that."
The truth is space
The game is…
Doubt.

That Light

There's a light that will shine,
It will beckon you come!
And like a feather to tar
You will stick.
An appeal so tremendous
It will zap your attention
Like a sheep to the slaughter
You'll go.
There's no power that pulls
But your own will that bends
And the thought that you make
"I must go."
Oh, how space is so dark,
Seems there's no place to go
Till that seducing light
Call for you.

Enamored

I, of flesh and bone, call earth my home!
This place, this very spot where I now stand
Is proof of that! You see it pulls and tugs.
Were I to jump I'd fall right back
And if I managed to go real high
Why, earth would just pull me right back
And I might land with a big splat!
Then if I died before this reading
The ground would call my name.
I would then answer with a fall
And as if that weren't close enough
A hole is dug that ties the knot
And then my friend…you can't be closer
To your home,
And don't complain and look in awe
Because this earth beckons for you…
As much as I!
It's not hard to feel enamored
With so much beauty about;
Oceans, deserts, forests, valleys,
Quite enchanting repertoire.
Mountains that meet up with heaven
As if trying to get away
While we humans court with Tierra
Maybe not completely knowing
That her game is to the death,
And we court her fruits of passion
Like the "hot lady" she is
Till the day we're mixed with Tierra.
Then she smiles and sighs "another"
And your name
Is on
That
List!

Cognition

Walking barefoot
I stepped on broken glass
red liquid flowed
for a moment
I realized
I was alive
…then, automaticity set in
and I was again myself.

July 17, 2001

The Garden

A symphony of color
Is what my garden shows,
The colors of the rainbow
Would not compare at all!
If you could color love,
If freedom's grace were painted,
The spirit in a child,
This three would dare compare to it!
This garden dwells inside us all,
Just till the soil
And it will grow.
As you add love to increase beauty
A harmonious mist of color
And bouquet of perfume
Mixed with Godly spirits will exude.

The Knock

Naked is the night without stars
Reminiscent of a garden without roses
Or a coupling without love.
Emptiness can fill and quench
Like flour a bowl of sugar.
Fear, fear is an unknown child;
It thrives and reigns supreme
Through ignorance survives
As understanding dies:
A crow comes to my abode,
A friend of old
Dressed up in black
Much darker than the night
A candle light upon my counter
Its flame a vigorous dancer
As through the open window blows
A crispy wind that wails a song!
My guests: The wind; the crow;
And something out there,
Something cold. A specter? Maybe
A disembodied soul.
At five till midnight I hear a knock,
More like a rasping on my door,
As if a synchronizing of events:
The crow; the wind; the disembodied soul,
And now a rasping at my door!
I said, "No more, no more!"
As one cold hand touched my wet brow
"Wake up!" "Wake up, your fever's down!"
And I, like Poe, wrote it all down.
His art like mine lives in our soul –
Our soul that never die.

August 21, 2001

Plight

In the morning of my discontent
As the sun's rays brought light to my home
And the plight that accosted my harmony
Was entombing a headache within my cranium walls
I reached out for the pampering cloth
That would soak in the liquid of life
From this sensitive temple of mine.
I strive towards life with death just steps behind
And by my side the memory of a bride
Whom just a day ago was buried
Yet lives inside my mind.
Were it not for the love, she'd be gone
And her essence would linger "no more!"
As I write she so tenderly
Caresses my brow

September 12, 2001

Ha!

Sit and waste a word,
Another…
Smooth, cool summer breeze.
Feelings of completed cycles,
enjoyment of life!
Realized to no-end "satisfaction"
and then "CRASH!"
No one there to read!
No one there to listen!
Where are you?
Where is my audience?
Ha! There you are.
Reading, listening,
moments of growth through words
not wasted, not wasted at all!

September 14, 2001

Reaching

Like a gift from the gods
Its spirit soars up towards the sky
And in its journey losing strength,
The Pine: A natural phenomenon.
With roots that dig into the ground
And spread tenaciously about
Impinging hard
As if the arms of a juvenile,
A repented and remorseful youth
Embracing a loved one.
A symbol of our nature,
We too hold hard
Spread out
And in the end reach out…
Reach out.

September 14, 2001

Enjoy

Banners of praise coming at me,
Duck or I'll be killed!
Silence reigns in tranquil hearts
And death is but an illusion.
Wake up! You Rock of Ages
Smell the soggy ocean kelp
Wet your noodle in a book
And read between the lines.
"Hogs are in the water!"
as I cradle Lasagna into my mouth.
Eyes that see need not listen,
"Do you see what I say?"
praise can maim as much as a gun,
a rose proves that,
as does divorce.
As for me, I live in our heart!
That blood drenched, muscle pumping,
Pumping wet liquid throughout you…
It's in your face now! Can you taste it?
Reading is so much fun.

As I Write

The minutes I spend writing thoughts with a pen
Using ink-type and paper to give life and sensation
That metaphor a creation that will quench hungry spirits
Now in search of salvation or a type of redemption
To questions unanswered while living a life
In this planet of ours that we think of as haven
A haven that's more like a trap.

Then we think it is not for a heaven does wait
Depending on our acts.
And we ponder for eons...
Or lifetimes let's say,
Till one day a small spark of creation
Taps our imagination
And thereafter we write with a knowledge not studied
Nor found in a book, rather born of the spirit,
My spirit, your spirit, creation alone!
As I write.

Dust

MORTALITY, such dreadful thought
Succumbing to such fateful end
Of living, dying and being
Dust...Again.

AGAIN, the cycle starts
Just when a child breathes life,
Cries, grows old, dies and life
Brings...death.

DEATH, seems to be the King by far.
Of man's unwished for end.
The Queen is Birth and we're just offspring
Playing...games.

GAMES, with high stakes
For to survive you must be sane.
To choose, to thrive, lest we give up before
Our...time.

TIME, that we have and make
For they who say "I have no time!"
Have somehow folded up their arms
Inviting...DUST.

Gray Notes

I Closed My Eyes

Like a repented Sodom was the world
a converted world
light as a feather.
I turned this way and that way
yet found no saltiness,
no vinegar,
a pure white light
blanket of love surrounded me,
healthy construction,
tall buildings, large bridges,
a zillion people
Happy? Happy!
"Wake Up!" I said.
My eyes opened
to reddish sun
and gunshots
mingled with sirens…
I closed my eyes.

February 10, 2000

Grow Old And Die

A fate imposed at birth
Conception marked the time,
Nine months a sheltered life
Then freedom gained advantage
And with it we grew bold
As bonds were cut
Mobility enhanced
Perception came in slow
As we, protruding, left our home
That fresh air gulp our spirit woke
And soon was second nature,
The birds, the sun, the cars
The smell of cookies in the oven
And Mom, she smelled the best.
We laughed and cried
For time, we did not care
Our toys, dad's lap
Those memories don't lie
Nor do they grow old
Grow old and die.

August 22, 2000

I Too Have Been Forgotten

Just like a breeze that passes by
Before you can say "There!"
A memory of long ago,
Wanted or not, exists.
And like a shadow in your head
Comes out to visit, so to speak,
And dwells for moments
Like a canvass picturesque
A long lost love
A best friend
The things we've had to lose
The times we proudly won
I, too, have been forgotten!
As a child long ago
No one to call me "cutie"
To hug me like before.
That part of me remains
Inside my mind.
Sometimes it passes through
Then, like a breeze
It is no more

The End

The End will come but once
No time to think
No time to say good-by
For in an instant
And with a flash
A spark,
A bang,
A bang to wake the dead!
That they may see,
That they may hear.
In death there is no glory.
"Salvation" that's the word!
The End, it comes but once
It's near
So close at hand
Reach out…He's there!
Quite fair to all
The End.

October 23, 2000

Wild Grass

Woods that smell of Battle Smoke
Wild Grass stained with red
As a white goose swims quite content
On a cool blue lake.

Three muskets lying on the ground
Each match a lifeless hand
Once joy and laughter filled those hearts
But not today!

Gray clouds announces a cleansing,
A baptismal of sort.
Cry the drums of righteousness, Cry loud!
You've taken many souls.

Oh! Winds of war, your shade is dark
As if in stealth you pass;
Your message is heard like a murmur –
Don't fight!

I thought the Bell's Toll was for me,
I heard it clear in battle.
When I got home my dear was dead
They buried her last night.

A patriot's life is colored gray
With tints of red, some white and blue,
But tears that come wash it all up and I insist
It's gray!

Sparrowgrass Poetry Forum
609 Main Street
Sisterville, WV 26175

My Wash

There the purple moon sat
As my wash dried in rain drops.
Five Bamboos were cut to the root
There were no stars that night
And the once cool breeze marred by a storm.

Once small sucker remained in my yard;
I persisted in letting it grow.
Yet the once lush surrounding perennials and grass
Now succumbed to a frigid bad air
That seemed to pervade and destroy.

One tall chute that kept coming
Looking different each time seemed convincing
Then it hurt the small sucker
And it dirtied my wash, and then it rained
Till I said, "that bamboo has to go!"

There the purple moon sat
As I cut that bamboo.
On the bad roots I poured liquid fluid,
Then I lit it and burned the damned roots.
Then the raindrops were gone
And my wash was my own.

Scheme Of Things

Deciduous is the tree
Whose leaves decide to fall
And in a moment
Completely bare it all,
As if in haste…they go!
Like the young man
Who leaves his home
And in his place a shade of dark
A saddening, a void!
Yet in the scheme of things
It was a season to depart
God knows!
There's yet another time
Another season
To come home.

January 31, 2000

The Cloud

It rained last night inside my bedroom.
The drops came sharp and heavy
Hurting as they touched my skin.
My momma said I should be patient
That this was not a heavy rain,
She knew, I think, of worst times.
Then, she placed her hand upon my brow
Instantaneously, like magic, the rain stopped.
My momma healed me often;
She knew how to stop the rain.
My clothes were drenched,
My room a mess,
And she that cared for me just smiled.
She'd dry my skin and tend my clothes
Until another dark cloud came inside
Appearing white and dry
Then gray, then dark.
That's when it rained again.
It filled the room until I drowned
And Momma was too late.

A Sigh Of Love

A Special Graduation

In a cool summer eve,
While the crickets and frogs
Orchestrated their tunes with delight
And a full moon made our silhouettes show,
When the fountain of youth
Mattered nothing at all
And the Magic of Life
Thrived within us,
Two bright eyes
Lit like stars
Looked straight at me.
It was my sister of two,
Ruffled hair, freckled face,
Just a little smudged-up from the playing.
Tiny hands reaching up
To the stars in the sky
As if saying, "I'll be there!"
With a smile so true,
(I'll confide that it runs in the family)
Well...I reached down to her
Threw her up in the air!
Well...She never came down...
She's a Grad. Here Today!

My Momma

Quite proud she looked at me
"Good Grades make me so happy!"
in a sweet, sweet voice
as she handed me a cookie
and placed two quarters in my pocket.
Looking at Momma was looking at love.
Heaven could not be heaven without my Momma
and Hell, well if you met my Momma
you would not believe such a place to exist.
"I love you" were the last words I heard
as I walked out the door,
nothing standing in my way.
I battled all in grade school
Bullies, Bad Teachers, Mean People;
they all fell like drops of rain
from an old beat up cloud
and I survived…Because of Momma,
My Momma, My Love.

March 1, 2000

Tempered Patience

That haberdasher man a canvass left
A three dimensional creation
An inspiration to all artists
Working oils in combinations
Blending styles to lure attention
Selling, selling their creations
For a cent that does not buy oil or paint
Not canvass, not a brush
But rags and maybe, maybe, half a bread.
That haberdasher man a canvass left
A hologram of life upon his death
It's on display inside my heart
Created with compassion, care and love.
The cost was death; the prize was life,
The brushstrokes made of sounds
And oils of tempered patience;
The canvass was my nature.
A magic touch was in this other brush
These strokes were "very special."
Oh Michelangelo was great as was El Greco
But papa's art was unsurpassed
His brush strokes dipped in inspiration
Of heavenly creation full of life
Not to be bought or cheaply bartered
But on display, a give to others!

Ponytailed Lass

Ponytailed lass what's in your mind?
The beauty of yesteryear's roses
the thorns they might have left behind.
Is the future what makes your eyes shine?
Ponytailed lass what's in your mind?
It is not hard to see your distinction
that you stand out quite bold
and your soul is your own
that a future is there for your taking.
Ponytailed lass what's in your mind?
There's a hurdle to run
and I hope without knowing you,
Ponytailed lass, that you're on it.

She Touched The Sky

Flamboyant she walked with ease of heart
In a long silk dress and shiny doublet top.
Her eyes like gemstone matched the sky
And in her bosom lay a dormant shiny spark
Of matter valued much by man as "Life!"
Her gait was straight, her pace was light
And Cupid's Arrow embedded in her heart.
She sang of love, of life, she touched the sky!
I reminisce these pictures of her life,
Her laugh, her thrust to survive.
I saw all this! "I" was that spark
Inside I grew, outside I was!
How could I not be part that?
A canvass pictorial I saved in my heart
Three dimensional with full color intact.
As I smell the perfume that's enchanting
And the thud of her boots on the dirt,
As the peppertrees bloomed
And the bees on frenzy for work
Thrives a memory that's everlasting.

Three Joys

The joys I have are three
Chris, Jenny, and Joshee
they bring me comfort, fun, and
responsibility.

I see in them my mirror image
and as my body folds and caves
they give me strength that comes like
waves.

When Chris swings bat and marks his hit
his eyes are full of electricity
and as he jumps and splendors off I charge
my battery up.

Oh, Jenny she's a toughie
princess all the way.
If she were queen of England there would
be hell to pay.

Josh is not to be forgotten
he's got wisdom up his sleeves
and settles right before the others push his
buttons.

As such are the joy of many, and
detriments of few
for me the love that comes
so plentiful and free is that which comes in
three.

August 23, 2001

Beauty

I met beauty last night
Standing on a broomstick
Piece of cake on one hand
Fish on the other
Dark bright eyes
Stood on one foot
Like a flamingo
A smile that could melt
The harshest character.
Me, I'm a marshmallow already.
Beauty jumped at me,
Hugging me, food and all!
I melted unto the ground
Giggling she said "pappy" –
Beauty is two years old.

That Feline

The feline stood still as I observed its every move
Then with a casual but uncanny movement
Its paw snatched at a rat trapping it
And toying with it, teasing it to escape!
Obvious of superior strength and speed
Rapid eye movement that followed every twitch
That "rat of a cat" would have quite a meal
Were it not for the shadow that watched
Quite observant and stealth.
In a trot it came out
Took one bit of that cat and the rat hit the road
As the cat meowed and scratched
Till the aggressor let go
Then it ran with one life less
And I hugged my pet doggie
For I loved him so much
When I was seven years old.

September 27, 2001

She Traveled Far

She came upon a midnight dreary
To ease a burden in her plight
Her eyes a dreamy green
And lips a sensuous red.
Her wholesome look and mannered ways
Could well depict her past
As I of flesh and carnal ways
To passion did give way.
Like a love that metaphors
I dwelled in a self-created bliss.
My love was hers, no questions asked,
Her love she gave to me.
We both lost time
For us, it just did not exist.
She traveled far,
Her road was thorny,
One thousand times she cried,
And that one night her spirit found
A love that freed her soul
And brought to me salvation.

Funtasia

January 16, 2000

Remember

I woke in a mysterious place
Where antlike dogs like horses ran
And canopies of rust-like metal
Pierced into a broth-like weather
Sharp drops of rain that soaked me
While the ground below me opened
To a gentle swarm of cow-sized hornets
That flew off and disappeared into the rain.
I walked five paces when I realized
There was no ground for me to stand on,
As I fell into a quick sand pond
With wild orchid plant-like fronds
That I so well remember!

All In One Act

I entered through a narrow chink
The curtain sharply lifting
Some shades of gray and black at first
Then a bursting band of colors
I felt so dignified and bold
To be so welcome at this show
My presence and attention beckoned
Obviously requiring my very unique presence
My own theater demanding my participation
Thus to feel an active member
Of this great actors' ensemble
'Tis a joy that's in my heart
From birth to Death all in one act.

May 20, 2000

"I'll Tell You What!"

I pulled a star the other night
So large and hot
I could not bring it home.
It was a sun
Much larger than our own.

I touched the moon one time.
I felt the little flag
Our astronauts left up there,
I did not pull it out;
My mom came in and I woke up.

I went inside our planet earth,
I found a lot of lava,
It runs like streams of water
Boiling hot.
Next time I'll put some in a pot.

The air is full of little creatures,
I put them in a box,
Then they complained too much.
I opened up
And let them run about.

Tonight I'm going to heaven;
I will talk with God.
He will need to handle war and crime
With a lot of love.

September 8, 2000

Colored Rocks

Last night I jumped quite high
I passed the sun and a few stars,
I ought to know, I felt the heat
    In my behind!

I saw a rainbow made of rocks,
A planet inhabited by dogs that talk
    And on my way to Xanadu
    I felt a water splash!

I crossed a giant planet
Much larger than our own
The inside full of custard,
    I had a belly full!

I went into a wonderful Galaxy
Where space was lighted up
And multi-colored rocks
That I just tossed about!

I woke up very early,
And laid still on my bed,
Then realized that the dream I had
Was no less real than my own room
Because "I" had been there!

Marbles

I've seen marbles of the prettiest kind
In a space immense and dark
Of various size and weight
They float as in a vacuum.
Some shine, quite bright
While others flicker on and off
There's one that's circled
By particles and dust
Another has a large black spot
But all in all the one I like
Is multi-colored all about
A haze of bluish-white and green,
It shines with warmth as if alive.
That is the marble I would buy.

August 20, 2001

Monopoly

Little men prevailing
Over a small piece of land
For principles and long gone ideals
Holding weapons in their hands!

Little men prevailing
Fighting other little men
In the name of some religion
By their God's dying in vain!

"Battle on, oh little soldiers"
Make your petty wars and die.
Someday comes a generation
That will not play in the mud!

Hearken to a spiritual freedom
That does not succumb to death.
Land and Traditions are trivial
"Greater", much greater is "man!"

Space

Space, the first frontier.
A habitat and home.
Where we begin
Then dwell and end,
And even then
The space is there,
Because, "we" occupy it.
I'd speculate,
Where it would be
If it were not for us?
As if "we" were the cause
Of this phenomenon.

September 1, 2000

Long Ago

I reminisce of yesteryear
When life was mine
My strength at peak
Adventures grand
And days were long
No end in sight
As "I", quite bold,
The wild beasts tamed
Large oceans swam
Tall mountains climbed
Grand deserts crossed
I wrestled dad!
And then one day
When feeling "real strong"
I tackled mom!
But that was long ago
When I was three
Today, I'm almost 10 years old!

April 3, 2001

Steel Glass Murals

Silver dust and molten graphite,
Pillars of Atlantean wrecks,
Majestic artifacts so gracefully resting,
Resting, resting in a rightful place.
Gulls and Pelicans stopped talking!
They were murmuring too much
Came a horseman from the heavens
In a flying metal stud.
Showers of a foreign x-wave
Showers, showers from above.
Golden arches and steel glass murals
Zero gravity for cruisers
In "a future from our past."
Choral, Algae, Lava Rock,
Beauty waves that whisper secrets
Of a Mystery that is not.

May 20, 2000

Volcano Warm

Fungus Covered Moss growing rampant
As Volcano Warm Springs birth water
Running endlessly then disappearing
Into forever thirsting ground crevices,
While two legged creatures rampage
Through lusciously green vegetation,
Malignant, medicinal and nutritious,
In a jungle pristine and full of life.

Like an elegant toy a vine hangs
From a tree of humongous proportions,
Marking delicious entertainment
As the water below, volcano warm,
Oozes with steam and minerals
While large predator creatures circle the air,
Sharp large bills with tiny teeth
And claw talons to pick up man size prey,
In a jungle pristine and full of life.

September 27, 2001

Nurtured In An Earth Tradition

Techno-Space Society
With Earth-type Café shops
In a large space-bound construction
Reminiscent of a mall.

A twenty-galaxy Market Place
That caters to one and all
With high-precision gadgetry
And some grand space food delights.

"In space there is no tomorrow
And your yesterday is here!"
Reads a sign upon the entrance
Of this grandiose space construct.

Nurtured in an Earth Tradition
Of a "Debtor-Credit-Plan."
Earth is but a mote in gamesmanship
But a mote is "Atom" strong.

Well-devised Teleport Stations
Of a 3rd Galaxy Creation
Makes the mall very accessible
Where all living organisms visit;
Buying, selling, trading, eating,
Just like humans at a mall.

Inter-Galaxian Portals
With a "3rd G" guarantee
Stamped upon the crystal handles
For all its users to see.

There's a Tadpole bug from Chuaw,
(Stands about three meters tall)
He insures for proper usage
And collects a standard fee.

Some "two legged" earthly beings
Don't believe this mall exists
They're lower than the 9th Galaxia
Lest they set their spirits free,

Then like gods they do prevail
As all Galaxians can attest.
Three earthly beings created:
Systems of exchange; Landscape;
Café Shops a la Mode,
In this Techno Space built mall.

Top of the peak on Mount Everest
Runs a clear beam to a Port,
Hasn't been used in a while
Because on Earth were too slow.

Technology to build devices
That makes space travel fast
Is not given enough freedom
Just covert study,

That's all!

Mixed Stokes

July 26, 2000

Baby

Huh! You're going to throw me up again?
And please don't squeeze me hard,
Those kisses that you give
Leave me feeling yuck!
Your hair is sort of in my face,
And clothes you wear
Smell awful sweet.
Often when you hug me
My tummy wants to groan,
Yet you're my main source
Of protection
From a way too dangerous world.
I enjoy your candid smile,
Your charm in cleaning me
And bathing my whole body.
They way you powder my behind
And care that I don't fall.
You feed me tenderly!
I feel your love
And dad's rough hugs
Are my delight!
I thank you for all that,
Your baby!

August 31, 2000

Kurillo's Juniper

Of Sun and Soil my nutrients come,
My runners tell a story!
A luscious green brings out my best
When liquid fluid my roots are fed.
I show quite well when I'm trimmed up
Five earth bound trees attest to that!
Quite proud they stand by me
A Juniper that adds that tint of green
To Golden Brown seducing trees
Surrounded by Red Berries
And like a stage: A corner place!
That thrives with admiration
"Poetic Nature" is the Theme
For this corner's ensemble

July 22, 2000

Unforeseen

A cloud upon leaving the Ocean
Felt sad and lonely
And as it cried
Its drops fell unto a lake.
The lake welcomed the drops
And the cloud was happy.
Actually it was happier
Than before
For on this lake
She found a home.

August 12, 2000

The Spirit

Beautiful like a pristine Forest
The waters of a newborn spring
And the colors of a rainbow
Such is the Spirit of Man.
Swollen with capabilities
Native to creations
Without mass or location
It thrives in a Godly state;
Such is its nature.

October 25, 2000

Rags Of Silk

A song of peace within a breath
Ten melodies to captivate my soul
Not quite the season I adore
Yet eloquent enough
For me!

Well dressed in rags of silk
A fragrance of fine cigars
And sweet perfume engulfs the air
I sit and wait not patiently
For thee!

Sweat trickles down my brow
Twelve fans are not enough
As something pulls my hair
Straight up like static.
Wake up!

A large crowd that sit like mutes
Like ghosts who cannot speak
And then a standing roar
The whole place shakes
Applause!

Again I feel a tug
My spinal chord reverberates
As from my chair I turn
My hand extends into thin air
So cold!

I hear my name three times
David, David, David!
Macabre and familiar sound
Of course I knew her well
My wife!

How elegant to dwell
In this enchanted ballroom
A soul that loves the art of song
Does very well
At haunting!

April 4, 2001

Ever-Present

Death is not a stranger
Ever-present and persistent
Like a shadow in stealth
It waits...
Patiently, covertly
For the thrill
Of a moment
A metamorphosis
Eloquent if not artistic
Unchallenged
It stands!
60, 70, 80
And some... untimely calls.
Unbiased by race
Unchallenged by sex
Respected by many
"Reaper of spirits"
Thy work
Is known.

August 2, 2001

Freedom

Haunted sand
Of paradise beaches,
Sacrificial
Sacred grounds.
Warriors knelt
To feed
Empty bellies
That growled.
Torches lit
The sand by night
As flowers
Were spread about.
Gratefully
They celebrated.
Honored,
And appeased
Their Gods!

Nay To All!

Morbid moments of displeasure;
Seconds before dawn.
Self tormented crucifixions
Of a non-religious sort.
There's no gallows waiting
Not even a sharpened ax!
Yet the body's crucial functions
Are just not up to par.
As if something "so disturbing"
"Sinister" and "evil"
Had its clutches
On one's soul.
Neither! Naught!
And Nay to all!
It is just the thought
Of "working"
That makes humans
Cringe and crawl!

September 26, 2001

My Love

My horse galloped on as rain fell hard on us both
And she that waited
Held my love.

Upon my path a horseman blocks my journey
And as I stop another,
And yet another.

The rain drops hard and in my heart
I know not fear
To mock my life.

"You let me be, I'll not repeat myself"
They did not budge
Nor did they speak.

And as the one behind me moved, for that which cuts a life
I drop my reins
For steel be in my hands.

Such dreadful fate, of those who choose to die
To die for naught
For naught is what they got.

The rain brought heavy drops, which merged with blood
Formed small puddles
In the mud.

And I, upon my horse galloped on
For she that waited
Was my love.

February 10, 2000

Two Larks

In the midst of euphoria
On a unknown terrain
Cried the Lark for its damsel
While two puddles, a large bush and ten trees away
Lay a man with an arrow stuck to his groin.
Twenty pygmies in hiding
Forty eyes well disguised in the bush
Watch with patience a body's last twitches
Slow and painless convulsion
Then, like general anesthesia the numbness sets in
In a world quite pristine, not like ours.
There's no sin here committed
Nor is there one to judge
As the small hunters jump out to the light.
Then they tie this Caucasian,
An Indiana Jones type of a fellow.
He had great aspirations to find hidden treasures
In places he'd not been before.
As they carried him much like a pig-on-a-stick
His mind wondered off, as he thought
That he'd make it to dinner tonight –
And that is when he saw
In a camp full of pygmies, a pot.
Then, a curtain of black
While two larks seemed to mate in the light.

Freedoms Of Grace

September 25, 2001

America United

Fly high, "Oh, Spangled Banner"
You're a symbol, "hardly won!"
Freedom for those who uphold you,
And have earned that Godly Right.
Freedom's not easy to come by,
With so many ruthless minds,
Trying to take over the world
By enslaving in their might.
The U.S. stands together,
United with open arms!
Just don't threaten Good Ol' Betsy
'Cause we'll die to set things right.
Which brings one more thing to mind,
Sleeping terrorists within;
"Wake Up" and you'll meet a Patriot
That may put you back to sleep!
As we stand through God United,
Not by Race or Sex or Creed
But by Freedom's Loving Grace
We shall set this world Free!

September 17, 2001

Shadows In Our Land

Two white doves flying high
on a Tuesday morning fall,
the culprit a sinister shadow,
that instilled, in stealth, a blow.
A third friendly's wing is broken,
a "Declaration of War!"
A vigil for all of the patriots
that were struck without a call.
Then, a gathering of Eagles
to consult with mighty God,
for there is a "Wrath of Justice!"
"Vengeance Is Mine!" cried the Lord.

March 4, 2000

Irish Noble Blood

In the open of a Mansion
Where I fought for life and soul
Using blades of hard worked metal
(That we poured our sweat to make)
Giving all my will in battle
Fighting for my King and Lord,
For it was my destined nature
To defend this Land and Throne.
Born a peasant in a kingdom
And of Irish Noble Blood
By the Oceans of my Fathers
Came the Thief to strip our pride
Take our Freedom then our loves.
"Hearken all you Sons of Ireland"
"Hearken all you Sons of God"
Cried my soul that raised my kinship,
While my hand the enemy slashed.
Dogs of War that come to pillage,
Knowing not whom they accost,
Let our blood show you true bravery
That does not a friend betray
In this Noble Land called Ireland
Where God once His spirit left,
As a token to His chosen
That His spirit dwells in them.

August 16, 2001

Offerings

Sweet were the apples of my youth
As I, in transgression devoured them
In the season of abundance.
While my father worked I fetched dessert.
My momma made things right
Sending the most delicious apple treats
To forgiving neighbors.
Smiling warmly they took the offering
And accepted my gesture of peace.

www.ingramcontent.com/pod-product-compliance
Lightning Source LLC
Chambersburg PA
CBHW062042290426
44109CB00026B/2704